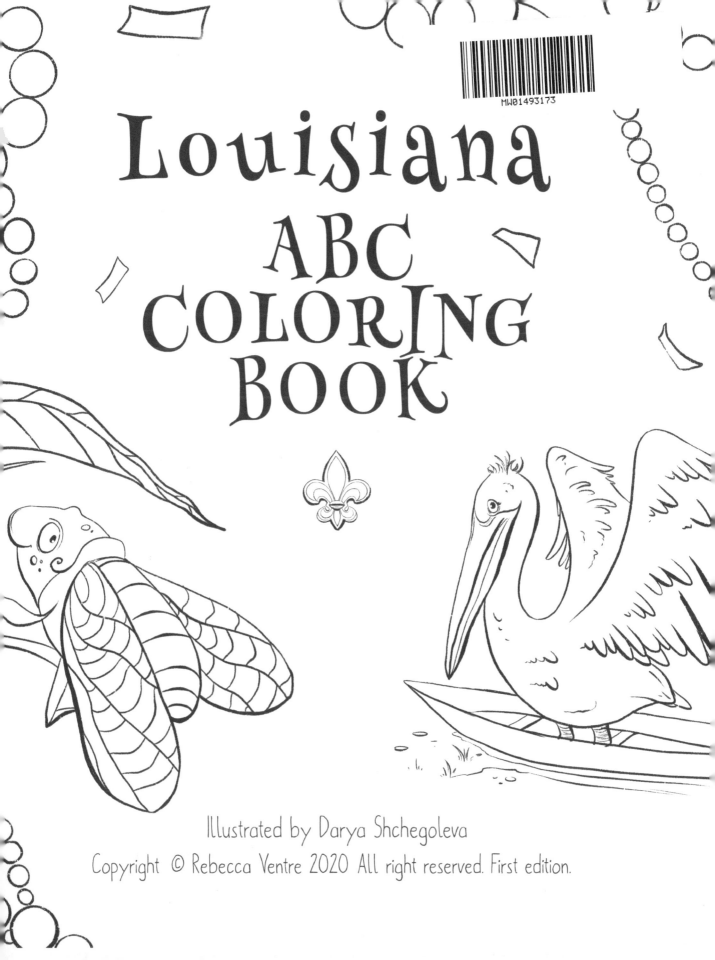

Louisiana ABC COLORING BOOK

Illustrated by Darya Shchegoleva

Louisiana Coloring Book

is for

ALLIGATOR

is for

BEIGNETS

Louisiana Coloring Book

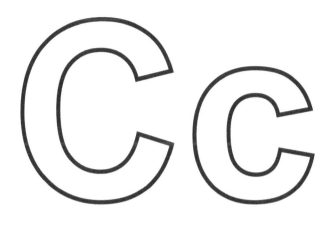

is for
CRAWFISH

Louisiana Coloring Book

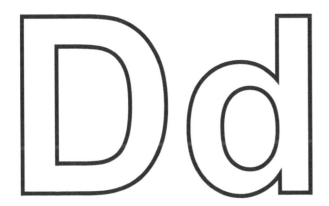

is for

**DOBERGE
CAKE**

Louisiana Coloring Book

is for

EGRET

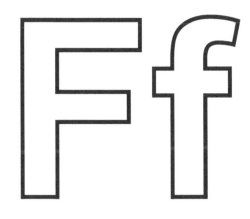

is for

FLEUR DE LIS

Louisiana Coloring Book

is for

GUMBO

Hh

**is for
HERON**

Louisiana Coloring Book

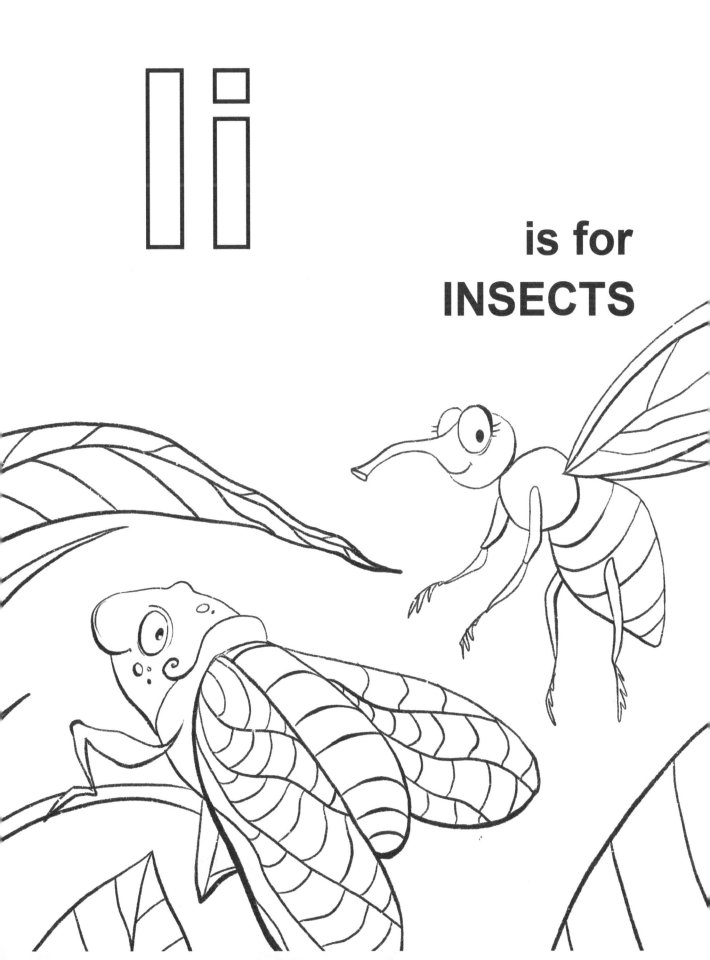

Ii

is for
INSECTS

Louisiana Coloring Book

Louisiana Coloring Book

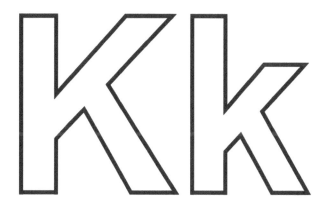

is for

KING CAKE

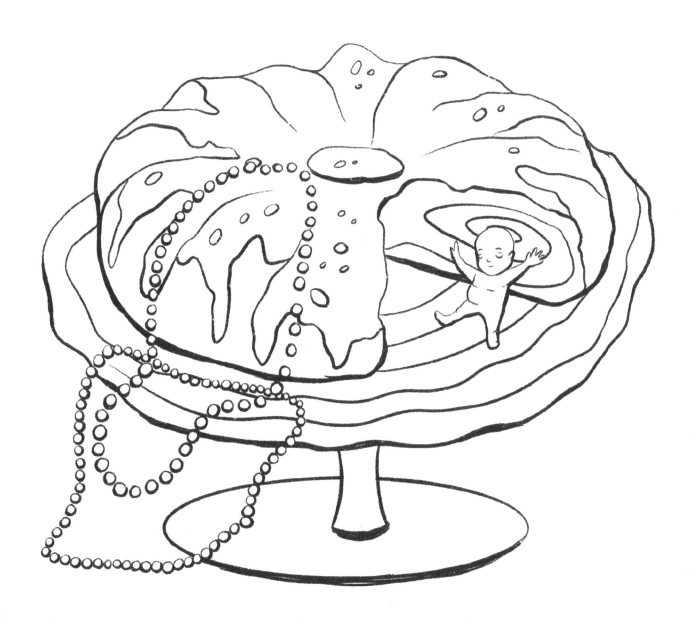

Louisiana Coloring Book

L l

is for
LET THE
GOOD TIMES
ROLL!

Laissez
Les Bon Temps
Rouler!

is for

MAGNOLIA

is for

NUTRIA

Louisiana Coloring Book

Oo is for OAKS

**is for
PELICAN
AND PIROGUE**

Louisiana Coloring Book

Qq

is for

QUEEN

Rr

**is for
ROUX**

Louisiana Coloring Book

is for

SNOWBALL

Tt

is for

THROW ME SOMETHING, MISTER!

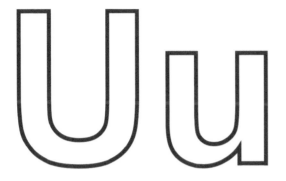

is for
UMBRELLA

Louisiana Coloring Book

is for
VIOLIN

Louisiana Coloring Book

is for

WASHBOARD

is for

GEAUX!

Louisiana Coloring Book

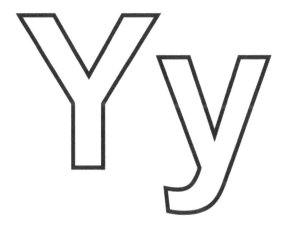

is for

YAM

Louisiana Coloring Book

Zz

is for

ZYDECO

Made in United States
Troutdale, OR
12/24/2024

27243574R00031